FAMINE, DROUGHT
AND PLAGUES

This edition produced in 1994 for
Shooting Star Press Inc
230 Fifth Avenue
Suite 1212
New York, NY 10001

Design:	**David West Children's Book Design**
Designer:	**Steve Woosnam-Savage**
Editor:	**Fiona Robertson**
Picture researcher:	**Emma Krikler**
Illustrator:	**Mike Saunders**

© Aladdin Books Ltd 1992

Created and produced by
Aladdin Books Ltd
28 Percy Street
London W1P 9FF

First published in the
United States in 1992 by
Gloucester Press

ISBN: 1-56924-057-4

Printed in Belgium

Natural Disasters

FAMINE, DROUGHT AND PLAGUES

JANE WALKER

SHOOTING STAR PRESS

CONTENTS

INTRODUCTION

Long lines of starving people waiting patiently for food have become a familiar sight on our television screens and in our newspapers. Many developing countries are susceptible to droughts and other natural disasters, which force these people from their land and homes in search of food and water.

We can do little to control the natural disasters that occur in these parts of the world. Yet there is much that can be done to prevent such disasters from producing widespread famine.

WHAT IS FAMINE?

Famine is the long-term shortage of food. It can lead to hunger and malnutrition, which is a condition caused by a lack of food, or by a shortage of those foods needed to stay healthy. Later, disease and starvation follow, and eventually death.

Famine is a widespread problem that can strike in any corner of the developing world. It affects countries that are unable to provide enough food to feed their population. Famine has been responsible for the deaths of many millions of people, and affects many millions more at any one time. In 1991, the United Nations estimated that 32 million people in Africa alone were at risk from starvation.

The principal cause of famine is drought, which is the continuous lack of rainfall. Famine can also result from other natural disasters, such as hurricanes, earthquakes, and plagues of pests. In 1991, a cyclone caused severe flooding in Bangladesh. The resulting famine and disease threatened the lives of an estimated 4 million people.

Humans can themselves bring about famine, for example through wars. During the Nigerian civil war in 1967-70, soldiers prevented food supplies from reaching Biafra Province. As a result, around 1 million people starved to death.

▼ Crop failure is a major cause of famine. As the rains fail, soils become dry and dusty. Drought, poor farming practices and the removal of vegetation help to explain the appearance of the kind of landscape seen in Burkina Faso, in Africa (below).

► During a period of famine, millions of people are forced to leave their homes in search of food. Like this family in Ethiopia (right), many flock to special famine relief camps where food aid is distributed.

◄ The photograph (left) shows the dried-up bed of the River Niger, in Mali, during the dry season.

WHAT IS DROUGHT?

Drought is a long period with no rain or with much less rainfall than is normal for a particular area. Almost one-third of the land on Earth is prone to drought, which affects more than 600 million people.

During a drought, the soil becomes parched and cracked. The hard-baked surface cannot absorb any water, and so very little moisture is retained in the soil. The dry and dusty topsoil is worn away by wind and rain, leaving behind patches of barren land.

Drought is a natural disaster that can affect any country in the world. However, its effects are made much worse in the developing world by a number of factors. They include overpopulation, overgrazing, and cutting down trees to provide firewood.

Hot, dry winds and very high temperatures, combined with a lack of rainfall and the evaporation of moisture in the ground, produce the conditions of drought. In some areas, periods of drought alternate with periods of flood, continually destroying food crops and farmland.

Hot, dry winds

Eroded topsoil

Dried-up wells

Failed crops

◄ Thousands of people are forced to stand in line for food after the failure of their crops through drought.

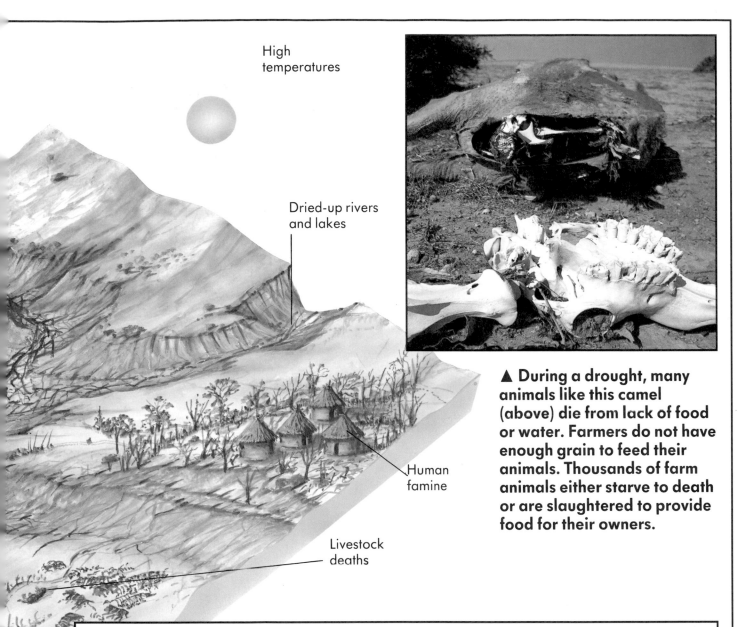

High
temperatures

Dried-up rivers
and lakes

Human
famine

Livestock
deaths

▲ **During a drought, many animals like this camel (above) die from lack of food or water. Farmers do not have enough grain to feed their animals. Thousands of farm animals either starve to death or are slaughtered to provide food for their owners.**

High temperatures
Unusually high temperatures can make water sources evaporate very quickly. Combined with a lack of rain, this can lead to droughts in areas that are not normally prone to water shortages. In 1988, temperatures in the fertile grain-growing regions of the United States soared to record levels. The drought that followed caused a large reduction in the grain harvest.

WHY DO DROUGHTS HAPPEN?

Droughts are frequently caused by natural factors, such as changes in weather patterns.

In 1982-83 the weather system in many parts of the world was dramatically altered by a phenomenon called "El Niño." El Niño was responsible for extreme weather conditions, including dust storms in Australia and drought in Southeast Asia.

Yet drought can also result from, or be made worse by, human activities. Trees help to keep soil fertile and to store water. When they are removed, the soil can no longer retain water. It becomes dry and dusty, and soil erosion sets in. As the land is deforested and overgrazed, it turns to desert. This spreading of desert areas is called desertification.

As warm moist air rises up from the oceans, it cools. Water vapor in the air condenses and turns back into water droplets, which fall as rain or snow. This process is called the water cycle.

Very high temperatures cause rain to evaporate as it reaches the warm ground. When air travels to the sheltered, or leeward, side of a mountain, it sinks down and heats up. Evaporation makes the rain clouds disappear, creating a rain shadow zone where little or no rain falls.

Water droplets evaporate and rain clouds disappear (rain shadow zone)

Dry air heats up as it sinks

◄ **Each year, many thousands of trees are burned to clear land for cash crops, which supply poorer countries with badly needed foreign currency.**

Water vapor condenses and forms clouds.

Warm, moist air rises and cools.

Rain and snow fall

▼ Hot, dry weather conditions in western Europe in 1976 caused widespread drought. Although its effects were serious, particularly for farmers, the drought did not result in famine.

El Niño

The winds and surface currents of the Pacific Ocean usually flow from east to west, carrying warm water to the western Pacific. A cool undercurrent of water flows back from west to east. El Niño occurs when these winds and currents change direction. The warm waters push closer than normal against the coasts of North and South America. They block off the upwellings of cold water that supply the rich fishing grounds off countries such as Ecuador and Peru.

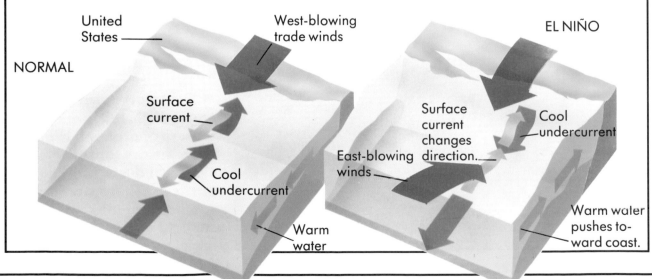

NORMAL

United States

West-blowing trade winds

Surface current

Cool undercurrent

Warm water

EL NIÑO

Surface current changes direction.

East-blowing winds

Cool undercurrent

Warm water pushes toward coast.

THE DAMAGE

In a drought-ravaged land, there are no supplies of food and water for the people, no water to make the crops grow, and no fodder to feed the animals. Hungry and weak, people are forced to abandon their land in search of food and water. Some travel hundreds of miles to food camps, or to the cities. In Nouakchott, Mauritania, over half of the population of 350,000 are refugees from the surrounding countryside.

In India, disaster can follow the failure or late arrival of the monsoon rains. When the rains failed in 1987, some 15 million Indian farmers had no work. About 192 million people across Asia were affected by drought.

The map below shows which areas of the world are affected by drought. It strikes mainly at the continents of Africa and Asia. Drought has been relentless in many African countries since the 1960s. Central and South America have also suffered periods of drought.

◀ Dust storms, such as the one in Mali, left, are a regular feature of drought. High winds blow the dry topsoil into thick clouds of dusty, swirling particles. These storms can be so thick that they shut out the sunlight and make daytime look like night.

▶ These people in northern Kenya are digging for water in a dried-up river bed. As water supplies run out, the only water left to drink is often contaminated. Dirty drinking water can lead to outbreaks of diseases such as cholera and typhoid.

 Drought-affected areas

▶ A disastrous drought affected Australia in 1983, resulting in numerous bushfires in the southeast of the country. A total of 75 people died in the fires, 8,000 were left homeless, and huge areas of farmland and forest were destroyed.

13

AMERICA'S DUST BOWL

Between 1931 and 1938, a major drought affected parts of the Great Plains in the United States. Severe dust storms swept through this area, which became known as the Dust Bowl.

One reason for the deterioration in the soils of this region was the planting of wheat on traditional grasslands. Unlike grass, wheat has shallow roots that cannot bind the soil to protect it from erosion.

As the drought set in and crops failed, fierce storms and winds blew away the dry topsoil in huge whirling clouds. Thousands of farmers and their families were forced to move to other areas, particularly to California.

United States

Mexico

Great Plains area affected by dust storms.

1930s Dust Bowl

▲ Homes, farms, cars, and machinery were ruined by the dust storms.

► The food shortages caused by the Great Plains drought affected the whole of the United States, causing food prices to rise dramatically. These people in Cleveland, Ohio, are in line for potatoes.

The map, below left, shows the Dust Bowl of the 1930s, and the surrounding areas that were affected by dust storms. Around 97 million acres of land in six different states were affected. The worst-hit state was Oklahoma.

Montana

North Dakota

Wyoming

South Dakota

Minnesota

Colorado

Nebraska

Kansas

Oklahoma

Texas

Dust storms

When topsoil becomes loose and powdery, it is easily swept off the ground and blown for hundreds of kilometers. Dust storms are common in the barren landscape of Burkina Faso (below), which has been stripped of vegetation in many places. The storms fill the air with huge quantities of hot, swirling dust.

WHAT ARE PLAGUES?

A plague is an invasion by large numbers of animals or insects. The animals often carry disease, and they eat enormous quantities of growing crops and stored grain. This can bring about a severe famine.

Some of the most destructive plagues consist of swarms of locusts. A single swarm may contain up to 50 billion insects.

Plagues of locusts have threatened several African countries in recent years. Rains in 1988 helped to relieve the drought. However, when combined with warmer weather, they provided ideal conditions for the locusts to breed. As a result, swarms of migratory locusts swept across North and Central Africa, destroying the much-needed harvest there.

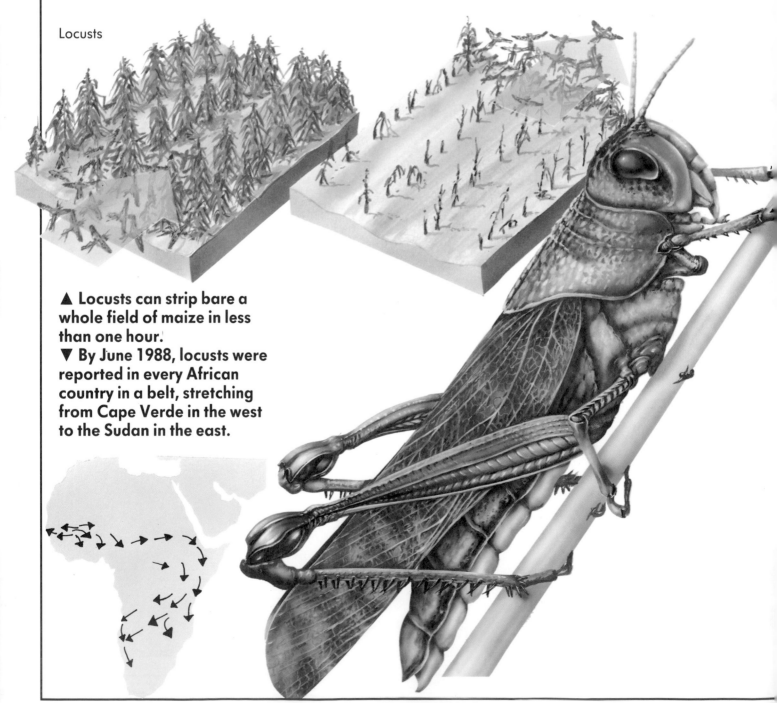

Locusts

▲ Locusts can strip bare a whole field of maize in less than one hour.
▼ By June 1988, locusts were reported in every African country in a belt, stretching from Cape Verde in the west to the Sudan in the east.

► Locusts fly thousands of miles in search of food. Locust invasions, such as the one in Dakar, Senegal, shown right, have plagued farmers throughout the world since ancient times. Locusts will eat any kind of vegetation, and can consume more than their own body weight of food in just one day.

▼ ◄ A locust is a type of adult grasshopper with wings. Its body is about 3 inches long. The female locust can produce hundreds of eggs in a single breeding season. As locusts become crowded and restless, they begin to migrate in swarms to other areas. The swarms can be so large, they block out the sunlight.

Kangaroos

Animal plagues can also involve large mammals such as kangaroos and goats. More than 3 million kangaroos are killed in Australia each year. Australian farmers consider that some of the 50 different kinds of kangaroo are pests. They feed and drink in the same areas as the farmers' sheep and cattle.

Controlling the kangaroo population has proved difficult as they cannot easily be contained by fencing.

FAMINE STRIKES

The effects of famine are often felt long after a disaster such as drought has passed. Many people, especially children and the elderly, become very weak from hunger and malnutrition. They begin to suffer from diarrhea and other famine-related diseases, such as kwashiorkor and marasmus. Their faces and stomachs swell up, and their legs and arms are frail and stick-like.

The threat of continuing famine is made worse when farmers fail to plant the following year's harvest. This happens either because all the seed has been eaten to avoid further starvation, or because the people are too weak to work on their land. Many may also have left their farms in search of food elsewhere.

▼ Short-term solutions to famine include the distribution of millions of tons of food aid to people in huge famine relief camps.

► Aid workers involved in the supply and distribution of food aid encounter many problems. Only foods such as grains and milk powder are suitable for famine relief operations because fresh foods will rot. A lack of roads and vehicles, as well as the problems of civil war and fighting, are just some of the other obstacles. The aid worker shown right is distributing ration cards to people in line for food.

Famine areas

The developing nations that are ravaged by famine are also among the world's poorest. One of the worst droughts in memory is now hitting southern Africa. Crops are dying and grazing lands are baked dry.

The problems of drought are made worse by the agricultural methods in these countries, which do not provide enough food to feed the population. There is no money to import food supplies from countries that have spare grain to sell.

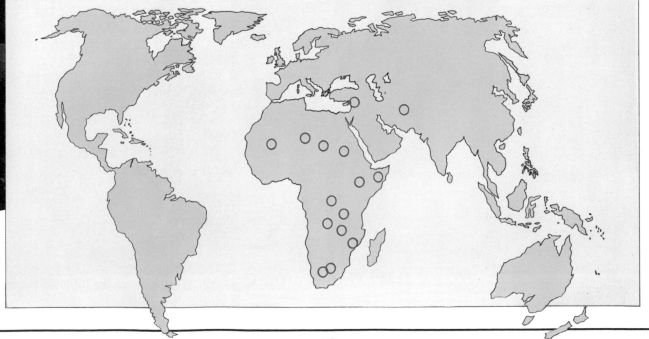

A HUNGRY CONTINENT

Two-thirds of the countries in Africa are affected by famine, caused principally by drought. Drought is a natural condition in the Sahel, where 90 percent of the rainfall is lost by evaporation. The drought problem is aggravated by overgrazing and deforestation. Both contribute to the spread of desertification. The town of Timbuktu in Mali, which used to stand in the fertile plains of the Niger River, is now surrounded by desert.

Overpopulation is a key factor of drought and famine. By 2010, the population of Africa will reach more than one billion. Yet even now, an area such as the Sahel produces less than 5 percent of the wheat needed to feed its people each year.

Many of the 100 million people in southern Africa depend on corn imported from South Africa. But the 1992 harvest will not even meet South Africa's own needs. Around 8 million tons of grain will need to be imported to avert a famine.

◄ In many African countries, the majority of the population live off the land. With so many mouths to feed, farmers can no longer leave their fields empty to allow the soil to recover. The soil gradually becomes overused and of such poor quality that crops will no longer grow in it. Overuse of the soil is made worse in countries such as Mali, left, by the chopping down of trees and other vegetation for firewood.

► The map on the right shows the drought-stricken areas of Africa. The Sahel region stretches for 3,000 miles from Senegal in the west to Sudan in the east. It makes up one-fifth of the African continent. Continuous crop failures in the Sahel have led to the deaths of 10 million people. The entire region of Southern Africa is also affected by severe drought.

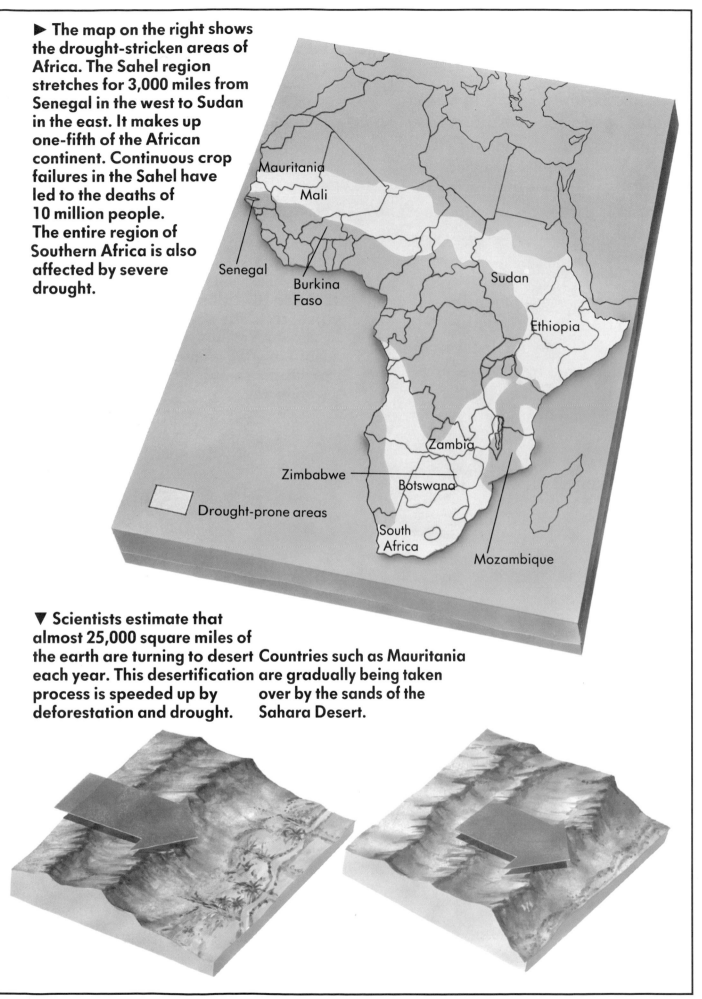

Mauritania

Mali

Senegal

Burkina Faso

Sudan

Ethiopia

Zambia

Zimbabwe

Botswana

Mozambique

South Africa

Drought-prone areas

▼ Scientists estimate that almost 25,000 square miles of the earth are turning to desert each year. This desertification process is speeded up by deforestation and drought. Countries such as Mauritania are gradually being taken over by the sands of the Sahara Desert.

PAST DISASTERS

Like present-day disasters, famines, droughts, and plagues in the past have been due to various causes. Rats brought plague to the Indian city of Bombay in 1898, killing around 12.5 million people. Flooding by the Yangtze River was responsible for the deaths from famine of more than 3 million Chinese in 1931.

Records of drought disasters in ancient times tell of famine in Egypt. When the annual flooding of the Nile River failed, the fertile farmlands were deprived of vital water supplies. Scientists have even discovered evidence of a drought that occurred in the United States more than 2,000 years ago, by examining the annual growth rings in the wood of old trees.

The first recorded plague occurred in Athens in the 1st century B.C. A plague in the city of Rome in A.D. 262 led to the death of 5,000 people a day. Biblical references in the Book of Exodus describe Egypt after a plague of locusts 3,500 years ago.

▼ A severe famine hit Ireland between 1841 and 1851 after disease destroyed the potato crop. The population was reduced by about 2.5 million through starvation and emigration. The picture below shows starving peasants begging for food outside a workhouse.

The Black Death

The plague known as the Black Death could be recognized by the black spots and swellings that appeared on people's bodies. It was a kind of bubonic plague, which is an epidemic disease passed to humans by rats. Between 1347 and 1351, the Black Death killed an estimated 25 million people throughout Asia and Europe, making it the greatest plague recorded in history.

The plague was brought to Europe by rats on board the spice ships that arrived from the East. Rats (below) are among the world's most destructive creatures. Each year, they consume vast amounts of the world's food crops.

FIGHTING DROUGHT

One of the principal aims in the fight against drought is to store as much water as possible during periods of rain. In Burkina Faso, curved lines of stones around fields prevent the run-off of rainwater and reduce soil erosion. Elsewhere, small dams made of soil help to retain the rainwater.

Slowing down the rate of deforestation is another important anti-drought measure. Trees soak in moisture like a sponge, releasing it slowly. They also add moisture to the air, as water passes out through their leaves in a process called transpiration.

To prevent the spread of the desert, sand dunes are anchored with brushwood fences and lines of fast-growing trees, like eucalyptus. The sand dunes around Nouakchott in Mauritania have been held down with branches, which also act as a windbreak.

In poorer countries solutions to combat drought include hillside terracing and the planting of trees such as acacia, which can tap water sources deep underground.

In Mexico, steep slopes have been planted with spineless cacti. The plants conserve the topsoil and provide food for animals during the dry season.

Trees act as windbreaks and stabilize sand dunes.

Water for irrigation can be pumped up from aquifers deep below the surface.

◀ **Without the water from irrigation, these crops on the Ganges Plain of India (left) would die.**

The process of transpiration
During the water cycle (see page 10), warm, damp air rises from the earth's surface into the atmosphere. Under normal circumstances, the air condenses into water droplets, which fall back to earth as rain or snow.

In tropical climates, up to three-quarters of the rains are lost through evapotranspiration. This is the process of water entering the atmosphere by evaporation, and by plant transpiration.

Water supplies can be conserved by building huge dams and reservoirs, which also provide hydroelectric power.

▼ **The Aswan High Dam in Egypt (below) provides water to irrigate the Egyptian farmlands all the year around. However, the dam holds back the nutrient-rich sediment that helps to make Egypt's soil so fertile. The dam itself is gradually filling up with deposits of silt.**

Crops should be grown in those areas that receive most rain. Livestock rearing is better suited to drier areas.

FAMINE AID

Without the aid efforts of international organisations working in famine-stricken countries in the 1970s and 1980s, the numbers of people dying from starvation and disease would have been even greater. In 1991, the United Nations World Food Program estimated that up to 20 million people depended on emergency food aid.

In the short term, famine aid involves bringing food supplies to affected areas to prevent people from starving to death. Inadequate transportation, poor roads, and war or tribal fighting are some of the barriers to the distribution of food aid.

In the long term, however, international aid must involve helping the economic development of poor countries so that they can increase their foreign earnings. These countries could then purchase equipment and technology from abroad, and also finance their own water management and other antidrought programs.

Machinery and farm equipment are donated by richer countries.

New deep wells are built.

Aid agencies provide the victims of famine with education and training, as well as with food and medical aid. Local farmers are encouraged to adopt improved farming methods. These include irrigation, contour plowing and growing more resistant crop varieties.

Relief trucks bring food supplies.

Cereals and other basic foods are distributed in the refugee camps.

Immunization prevents the spread of disease.

Aid workers encourage self-help among the local population

► In 1992, over 1.25 million tons of overseas food aid will be needed in Ethiopia to avoid the deaths of 7 million famine victims. Trucks and fuel supplies are also needed to ensure that the food aid reaches the famine areas.

Food storage and processing facilities need to be improved to reduce the huge quantities of grain lost after each harvest. More than 70 million tons of key cereals, such as rice and corn, are lost every year.

Improved farming methods are introduced.

Planning ahead
In the picture below, millet seed is being distributed to the villagers of Tchawai village, near Bokoro, in Chad.

Economic policies for the future must concentrate on producing more food crops for the country's own population, rather than cash crops.

WHAT CAN WE DO?

Although droughts and famines cannot be completely wiped out, certain measures can be taken to reduce their impact.

The production of traditional crops, such as yams, sweet potato, and cassava, is being increased. A new bread has already been developed, which is made from cassava or sorghum flour instead of wheat flour. New farming methods and crops can encourage people to find their own solutions to the drought problem, without having to leave their land.

Modern technology helps to control pests such as locusts, which breed in huge numbers in warm, damp conditions. When satellite pictures show significant rises in the moisture levels of their breeding grounds, these areas are sprayed with pesticides. Scientists have also used computers to establish a link between ocean temperatures and drought. With this method, they predicted accurately the recent droughts in the Sahel and in northeastern Brazil.

Since the 1970s, aid agencies and numerous charities in the developed world have raised millions of dollars to fund their aid programs. The money has come as a result of frequent advertising campaigns, appeals for money, and huge fund-raising efforts. Their work has helped to increase our awareness of the suffering of famine victims and of the problems they face.

► In Ethiopia, the government has organized thousands of farmers to build dams and dig terraces that help to retain rainwater. In the photo, right, trees are being planted to protect newly created earth dams, called diguettes.

◄▼ Education and training, such as this practical mechanics course shown left in Dakar, Senegal, are important aspects of any program to aid economic development.

Population growth

In many developing countries, the rate of population growth is so rapid that there are too many mouths to feed. In Bangladesh, one of the world's most densely populated and poorest countries, about 7 babies are born every minute.

Controlling the growth of the population is a key issue in the fight against hunger and famine. These women in Calcutta, India (below), are learning about a government campaign to reduce the number of babies born each year.

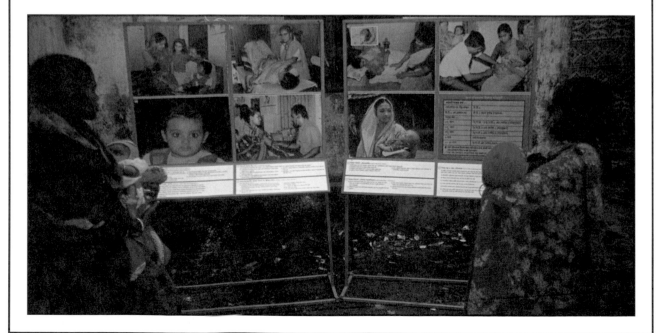

FACT FILE

Population growth

About 90 percent of the world's population growth occurs in the developing world. The world's population is increasing by 80 million each year. By the year 2070, the population of the world will have reached 10 billion people.

United Nations

The World Food Program (WFP) of the United Nations gives priority aid to poor countries with food shortages. It has recently funded projects to stop desertification in Burkina Faso, to undertake water supply and reforestation work in India, and to conserve soil and water in Haiti.

A plague of birds

Millions of red-billed queleas, which are tiny sparrowlike birds, fly across Africa each year. They swoop down on the ripening crops, consuming thousands of tons of rice, millet, and wheat.

Agriculture in India

In 1978, drought affected two-thirds of India, when less than 60 percent of the expected rainfall fell in the worst-hit areas. A famine disaster was avoided because of new farming techniques introduced during the 1950s and 1960s. During this so-called "green revolution" in Indian agriculture, irrigation became more widespread.

Also, new types of wheat and rice that produced higher yields were grown. Stockpiles of food surpluses averted the threat of famine.

Recent disasters

1990

Spain — the most severe drought since 1945 affected parts of Spain. Irrigation was banned in the southwest of the country, and water rationing was introduced in the Basque region in the northeast.

Jordan — emergency food relief was needed for almost half a million refugees who had fled from Kuwait and Iraq following the Iraqi invasion of Kuwait.

Ethiopia — government and opposition soldiers agreed to open up the Red Sea port of Massawa to let in U.N. ships carrying relief supplies. Food aid was needed for the 4 million people starving in the provinces of Tigre and Wollo.

1991

Africa — the famine situation was judged to be critical in Angola, Ethiopia, Mozambique, Somalia, and Sudan. In all these countries, the problems of food distribution were made worse by civil war.

1992

Mozambique — drought in six of the country's provinces led to serious grain shortages. The civil war prevented the cultivation of food crops and the adequate distribution of food supplies. One million refugees fled into neighboring Malawi, where harvests were also badly affected by drought.

Botswana — with only one-fifth of the normal crop area planted this year, grain will be in short supply and food prices will rise. In a country where an estimated 1 in every 4 children suffers from malnutrition, large quantities of cereals will have to be imported to avert famine disaster.

Somalia — on January 12, the water supply in the capital, Mogadishu, was cut off, and thousands of tons of food aid in the city's port were looted. Hundreds of thousands of refugees in nearby camps were on the brink of starvation. Around 700 Somali refugees a day were flocking into neighboring Kenya. Fighting between rival groups has continued in the capital since November 1991.

Deforestation

In the Indian state of Maharastra, deforestation is blamed for drying up the water supplies in a total of 23,000 villages. Deforestation in the Ethiopian Highlands has reduced the amount of water flowing into the Nile River. This has disastrous consequences for the many farmers who use the river's water to irrigate their farmlands.

GLOSSARY

aquifer – an underground reservoir of water. It is formed out of porous rocks, such as sandstone, that hold water.

atmosphere – the layer of gases that surrounds the earth.

bubonic plague – a disease that causes swellings under the skin. It is passed to humans by rats and other small animals.

cash crop – a crop that is grown to be sold, and not to provide food for local people.

condense – when a gas, such as water vapor, cools and turns into a liquid.

deforestation – the removal of trees from a landscape.

developing country – a poor country that is trying to improve its economy and give its people a better way of life.

drought – a long period of dryness with a continous lack of rainfall, or with less rainfall than usual.

Dust Bowl – an area of the Great Plains that suffered a severe drought in the 1930s.

dust storm – swirling clouds of fine sand, dust, and topsoil that are blown off the land.

El Niño – a reversal in the direction of winds and ocean currents that causes dramatic changes in the world's weather. It is named after the Spanish word for "Christ child," since it usually occurs around Christmas time.

evaporate – when a liquid, such as water, is heated and turns into a gas or vapor.

famine – a long-term shortage of food supplies.

fertile – describes land on which healthy crops will grow.

food aid – the supply and distribution of food to famine victims.

irrigation – the artificial watering of crops in dry areas.

malnutrition – a condition caused by a lack or shortage of healthy food.

monsoon – a warm wind that brings heavy summer rains to parts of Asia.

overgrazing – when too many animals graze on grasslands and destroy the vegetation that grows there.

overpopulation – when too many people live in a country that cannot produce enough food to feed them.

pesticide – a chemical that is sprayed onto crops or land to destroy certain insects and other pests.

plague – an invasion by large numbers of animals. "Plague" also means an epidemic disease that kills large numbers of a population.

reforestation – replanting forests in an area where trees have been cut down.

satellite – a type of spacecraft that takes photographs and other measurements of the earth while orbiting around our planet.

sediment – a mixture of soil and tiny pieces of rock that are carried along by a river.

soil erosion – the removal of topsoil by wind and rain.

transpiration – the process of plants giving off water, mainly through their leaves and stems, into the atmosphere.

water cycle – the continuous movement of water from the earth's surface, up into the atmosphere, and back down to the surface.

INDEX

Photographic credits:
Cover and pages 7 top, 8, 9 bottom, 11, 13 bottom, 15 top, 16, 20 top, 27 top and 29 bottom: Frank Spooner Pictures; title page: Natural History Photographic Agency; pages 4-5, 9 top and 13 top: Eye Ubiquitous; pages 6-7, 7 middle, 10, 12, 17, 21, 22, 24, 27 bottom, 28 and 29 top: Panos Pictures; pages 15 bottom and 19 bottom: Bruce Coleman Limited; page 18: The Hulton Library; page 19 top: Mary Evans Picture Library; page 20 bottom: Popperfoto; page 25: Spectrum Colour Library.